To each and every EXPERT – to those parents, grandparents, teachers, librarians, carers, child development specialists, paediatricians, obstetricians, nurses, child psychologists, health educators, clergy and psychoanalysts who read over and looked over our work, talked to us, taught us, and corrected us over and over again as we created this book for young children. We could not have created this book without you. THANK YOU! – R. H. H.

For Eva and her parents, Jenn and Fred
N. B. W.

WALKER BOOKS
AND SUBSIDIARIES
LONDON · BOSTON · SYDNEY · AUCKLAND

First published 2013 by Walker Books Ltd
87 Vauxhall Walk, London SE11 5HJ

2 4 6 8 10 9 7 5 3 1

Text © 2013 Bee Productions, Inc.
Illustrations © 2013 Nadine Bernard Westcott

The right of Robie H. Harris and Nadine Bernard Westcott to be identified as author and illustrator respectively
of this work has been asserted by them in accordance with the Copyright, Designs and Patents Act 1988

This book has been typeset in Berkeley Old Style and Handwriter

Printed and bound in China

British Library Cataloguing in Publication Data:
a catalogue record for this book is available from the British Library

ISBN 978-1-4063-4931-3

www.walker.co.uk

What's In There?

All About Before You Were Born

Robie H. Harris

illustrated by

Nadine Bernard Westcott

New babies begin to grow in a special place inside a woman's body called the uterus. That's where you grew before you were born. That's where everybody grew before they were born.

Girls and women have a uterus. The uterus is just below a girl's or woman's tummy and is very soft and stretchy. Boys and men do not have a uterus.

All growing babies begin as one tiny cell. Half of this cell comes from a woman's body. The other half comes from a man's body. Together, they can grow into a baby.

When a growing baby is inside the uterus and is only a few days old, it has already grown into a ball of cells. That ball is the size of the teeniest, tiniest dot – about the size of a pencil dot.

uterus

growing baby

Soon, the growing baby is about the size of an apple seed. Its backbone has started to grow. And its heart has started to beat. It has a tiny tail and looks a lot like a tadpole.

The whole time a growing baby is inside a woman's uterus, it floats in warm water. The water all around the growing baby keeps it warm and safe from bumps and pokes.

Then the growing baby grows even more. Soon, it is about the size of a big peach.

Now it has eyes, ears, lips, arms, fingers, legs, toes – and a nose! Its bones and muscles are growing. Its tail has begun to disappear, and it is beginning to look more like a baby.

Now the growing baby has the special part that will make it a girl or a boy − a vagina for a girl and a penis for a boy. Soft, fuzzy hair covers its whole body! And its fingernails and toenails have started to grow.

When a growing baby is inside a woman's uterus, food and drink and air go into her body. The food goes into the woman's tummy, where it breaks into very, very tiny bits of food.

Our growing baby must get really hungry while it's doing all that growing in THERE.

Do you really think our baby eats and drinks in THERE?

Then those tiny bits of food and the drink and air pass through a special twisty tube right into the growing baby's body – and help the baby to stay healthy and to grow bigger and stronger.

mouth

PICK YOUR OWN

tummy

uterus

twisty tube

growing baby

Soon, the growing baby is about the size of a small pumpkin. Now it can hear noises, like when a doorbell rings *ding-dong!* or a person sings "La-la-la-laaaaa!". And it can make noises – even hiccups and burps.

It can also see light. And it can kick, punch and somersault.

Now the growing baby's lungs are pushing in and out. It's practising how to breathe. And it's growing eyebrows and eyelashes and hair on its head. It can open and close its eyes. It can suck its thumb and sleep.

To make more room for the growing baby, the woman's uterus and skin stretch and grow bigger – the same way a balloon stretches and grows bigger.

Sometimes, the baby drinks the water it floats in and pees a little bit. But most growing babies do not poo inside the uterus.

After growing for a very long time – nine whole months – the growing baby is about the size of a watermelon.

Now its tummy, brain and heart – and all the other parts of its body – are working very, very well. And it's big enough, and strong enough, and ready to be born.

When a new baby is ready to be born, its mummy's muscles squeeze and push the baby out of her uterus.

Soon the baby comes out through a stretchy opening between its mummy's legs called the vagina. And the baby is born! Most babies let out a cry the moment they are born.

Sometimes, the doctor makes a special cut into the mummy's uterus and lifts the baby out. And the baby is born! Then the mummy's cut is sewn up with a special thread. The cutting and sewing do not hurt the mummy or the baby.

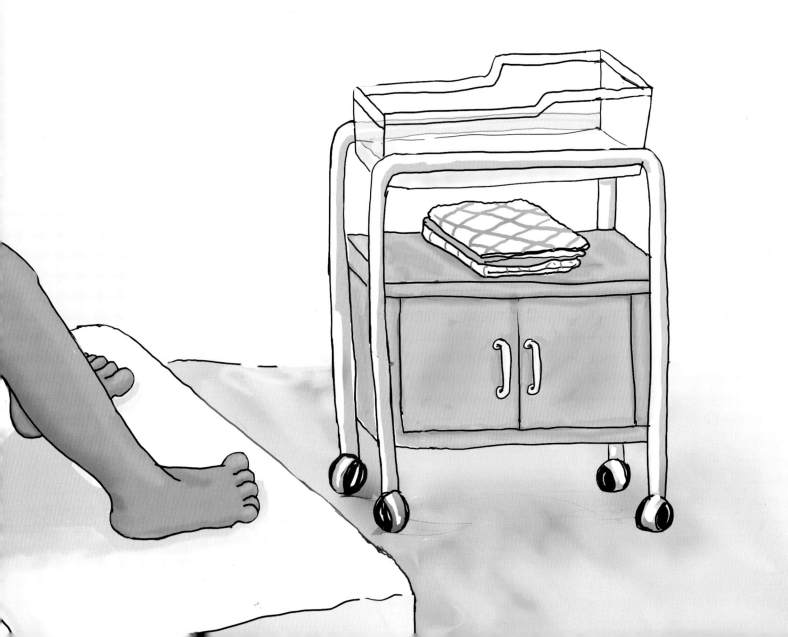

As soon as the baby is born, the doctor or midwife cuts the twisty tube. This cutting does not hurt the baby or the mummy.

Your bellybutton is where the twisty tube was attached to you when you were growing inside the uterus.

A few moments later, the baby is wiped, dressed in a nappy, babygrow and hat, and wrapped in a soft blanket.

Brand-new babies can do a lot of things. They can look, suck, yawn, burp, fuss, cry and sleep.

Cuddling, holding, kissing and even looking at a new baby feels wonderful. So does whispering, talking or singing to a new baby.

Saying, "I love you!" to a baby feels wonderful too.

Sometimes when babies are born, two or even more babies come out. These two babies are called twins. Some twins are two girls. Some are two boys. Some are a girl and a boy.

When three babies come out, they are called triplets. And sometimes – but not very often – when babies are born, four or five or six babies come out.

But our gerbil babies were a whole lot tinier than our new baby, Jake.

All babies are born into or adopted into their family. And the day a baby is born is that baby's birthday. Every baby's birthday, and child's birthday, and grown-up's birthday, is a very, very special day.

Everybody was a baby once. Even you!